Wedges

BY KATIE MARSICO • ILLUSTRATED BY REGINALD BUTLER

The Child's World

Published by The Child's World®
1980 Lookout Drive • Mankato, MN 56003-1705
800-599-READ • www.childsworld.com

Acknowledgments
The Child's World®: Mary Berendes, Publishing Director
The Design Lab: Cover and interior design
Amnet: Cover and interior production
Red Line Editorial: Editorial direction

Photo credits
Alexey Laputin/Shutterstock Images, cover, 1; Dianne
McFadden/Shutterstock Images, 9; Shutterstock
Images, 10, 12, 19, 20; Rob Cruse/iStockphoto, 17;
Dmitriy Shironosov/Shutterstock Images, 23

Design elements: In.light/Dreamstime

ISBN 9781614732778
LCCN 2012933658

Printed in the United States of America
Mankato, MN
July 2012
PA02120

ABOUT THE AUTHOR

Katie Marsico is the author of more than 100 children's and young-adult reference books. She uses wedges to keep the doors in her house open. These simple machines help her stay aware of what her kids are doing.

ABOUT THE ILLUSTRATOR

Reginald Butler is a professional artist whose work includes poetry, painting, design, animation, commercial graphics, and music. One day he hopes to wake up and read his comic in the paper while watching his cartoon on television.

Table of Contents

Tools and Machines

What would your life be like without tools and machines? You use tools and machines every day. Tools and machines help you do **work**. Computers are machines that help you store information. Cars are machines that help you move from place to place. Washing machines help you clean your clothes. These kinds of machines have many moving parts. Machines with many moving parts are **complex**. Complex machines are made up of many simple machines. There are six types of simple machines. They are wedges, inclined planes, screws, levers, wheels, and pulleys. Let's see how wedges make work easier!

You probably use simple machines every day.

The Work Wedges Do

A wedge is a type of inclined plane. An inclined plane is a slanted surface. It helps people raise or lower things from one level to another. Objects move up or down an inclined plane. The inclined plane doesn't move.

Wedges are also slanted surfaces. Wedges have a wide base that slopes to a thin edge. Wedges move into or against another object to **split** the object. People also use wedges to hold an object in place.

Wedges help split things, and inclined planes make it easier to bring things to a higher level.

Split It

You have probably used a wedge to split something. Picture the sharp points of a fork. These points are wedges. You separate your food into pieces when you push the points of the fork into your food.

WEDGES IN THE SKY

Have you ever flown in an airplane? You may have noticed the airplane has a pointed nose. This is actually a wedge that makes it easier for the plane to move through the air!

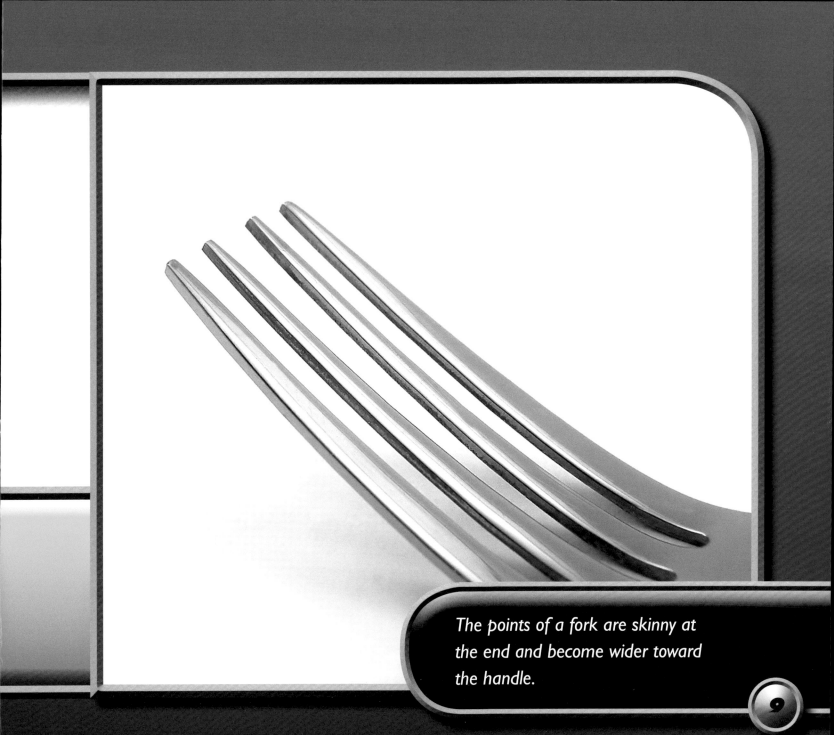

The points of a fork are skinny at the end and become wider toward the handle.

The blade of an axe makes it easier
to split wood into smaller pieces.

The blades on knives, shovels, and axes are also wedges that help split things. So are your teeth! You usually place force on the wide part of a wedge. This drives the pointed end into the object you are trying to split.

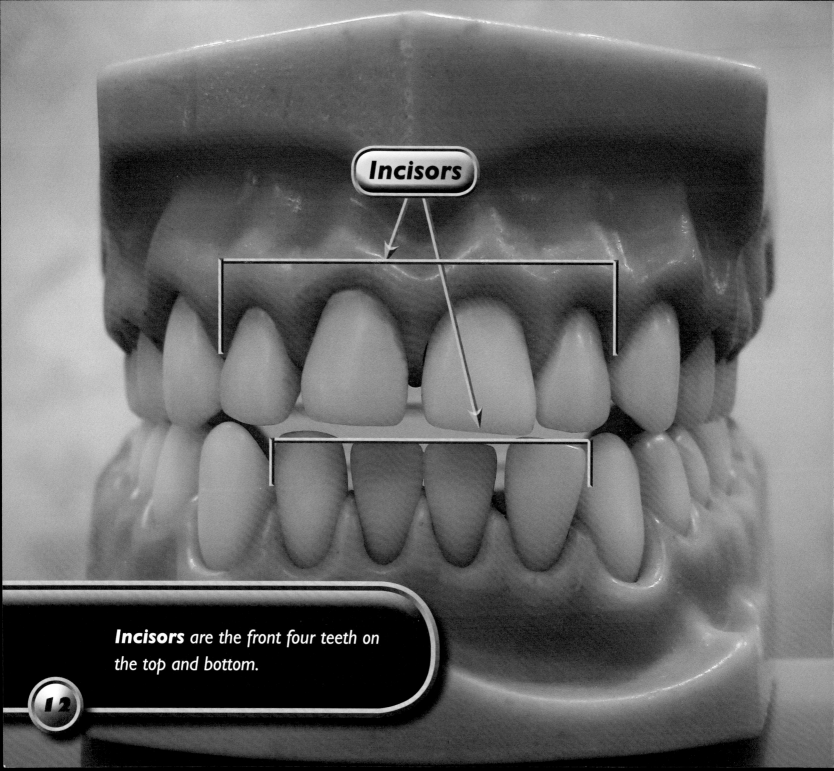

Incisors

Incisors are the front four teeth on the top and bottom.

12

Think about your teeth to get a better idea of how wedges work. Imagine you are eating steak. You use your fork and knife to cut the meat into small pieces. But the little bits of steak need to be even smaller for you to swallow.

Luckily you have teeth called incisors. You place a forkful of meat into your mouth and start chewing. Your incisors push into the steak. These teeth split the meat. Would you have guessed that you have simple machines inside your mouth?

Hold It Open

A wedge can also hold something in place. Doorstops and some bookends are examples of this type of wedge.

How do these wedges work? They create **friction**. Friction happens when two objects rub together. The objects then slow down or stop. Take a closer look at a doorstop to see how a wedge holds something in place.

Some bookends are wedges and help hold books in place.

15

There is often a little space between a door and the floor. This makes it easier for the door to swing open and shut. But the door and floor do not rub against each other to create friction. The door might not stay open on its own.

You can push the pointed part of a doorstop underneath a door. Friction is created between the bottom of the doorstop and the surface of the floor. This stops the door from closing.

The doorstop keeps this door propped open.

Thick or Thin?

Not all wedges look alike. They do not all work the same way either. A thick, short wedge will help you split something faster. But you need to push on the wedge with more force to drive it into the object.

An axe with a thick blade needs more force than a thinner axe blade would need to split something.

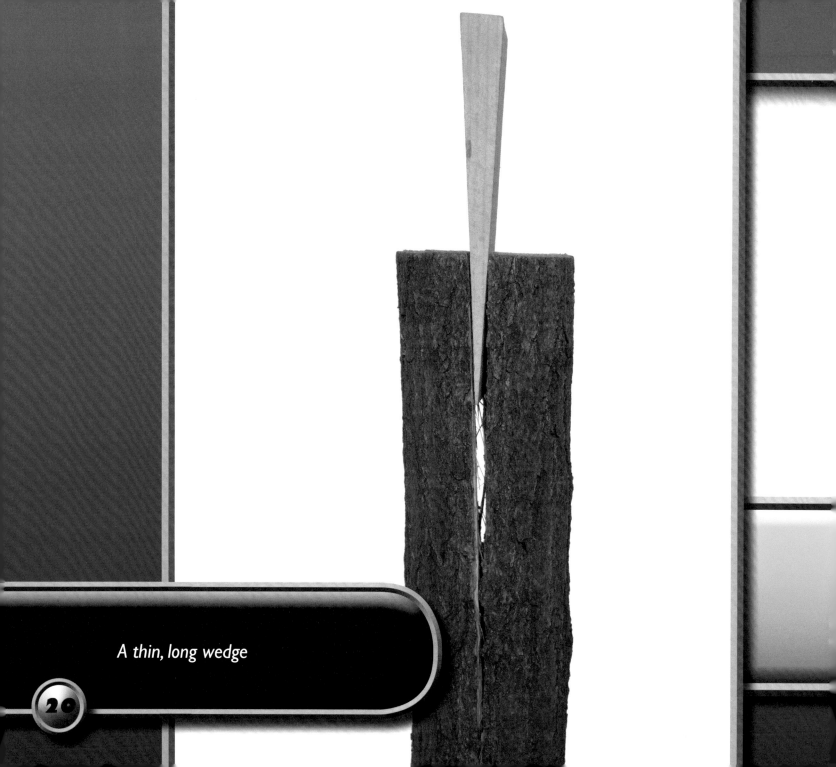

A thin, long wedge

You use less force to split something using a thin, long wedge. It takes longer though. The thinner wedge has to travel farther inside an object before it makes the object split.

EARLY PEOPLE'S WEDGES

Humans have worked with wedges (besides their teeth) for about 2.6 million years. Early people used stone axes to cut meat and firewood.

Wedges Everywhere

Now you know about wedges. These simple machines are everywhere! They are on your kitchen table and inside your family toolbox. Wedges help you chew your food and keep doors from swinging shut. They make it easier to split objects and to hold them in place. How will you use wedges today?

A chef uses a wedge—a knife blade—to slice a tomato.

GLOSSARY

complex (kuhm-PLEKS): If something is complex, it has a lot of parts. A computer is a complex machine.

friction (FRIK-shuhn): Friction is the force that slows down objects when they rub against each other. A wedge underneath a door can create enough friction for the door to stay open.

incisors (in-SYE-zurs): Incisors are narrow-edged teeth in the front of the mouth that are used for cutting food. Incisors are wedges.

split (SPLIT): If things split, they are broken apart by force. People use wedges to split wood and other things.

work (WURK): Work is applying a force, such as pulling or pushing, to move an object. You do work when you use a wedge to split something.

BOOKS

Bodden, Valerie. *Wedges*. Mankato, MN: Creative Education, 2011.

Christiansen, Jennifer. *Get to Know Wedges*. New York: Crabtree Publishing Company, 2009.

Gosman, Gillian. *Wedges in Action*. New York: PowerKids Press, 2011.

WEB SITES

Visit our Web site for links about wedges:
childsworld.com/links

Note to Parents, Teachers, and Librarians: We routinely verify our Web links to make sure they are safe and active sites. So encourage your readers to check them out!

INDEX